The Absenc

A Presence Below:

Re-Envisioning

Centralia, Pennsylvania

John G. Sabol
C.A.S.P.E.R. Research Center

Also by John Sabol

Ghost Excavator (2007)

Ghost Culture (2007)

Gettysburg Unearthed (2007)

Battlefield Hauntscape (2008)

The Anthracite Coal Region (2008)

The Politics of Presence (2008)

Bodies of Substance, Fragments of Memory (2009)

Phantom Gettysburg (2009)

Digging Deep (2009)

The Re-Haunting(s) of Gettysburg (2010)

The Haunted Theatre (2011)

Ghost Culture Too (2012)

Beyond the Paranormal (2012)

Digging-Up Ghosts (2nd publishing, 2013)

Burnside Bridge (2013)

The Gettysburg Experience (2013)

The Absence Above, A Presence Below:
Re-Envisioning Centralia, Pennsylvania

Ghost Excavator Books, Inc™©

Bedford, Pennsylvania, USA

ISBN-13: 978-1490912233
ISBN-10: 1490912231

Ghost Excavation Books, Inc. ™©
A division of C.A.S.P.E.R. Research Center™©,
Bedford, PA, USA
www.ghostexcavation.com

<u>Preface</u>

"Out of the sinister caverns of Night

Out of the depths where the Hell-fires are glowing

Cometh a cry, floating up to the Light....

Give us, in God's name, our wages of Bread!"

- **Robert Buchanan**

The daily "Bread" in Centralia is no more. It has been replaced with "Burnt Offerings". These offerings are not enough to "offer" the contemporary visitor, so a different vision of a coal-mining town has emerged from the depths of the earth. This vision is a popular one, but one that is inadequate, and sometimes false.

A definition is a simple route to an explanation: coal mining is the process of extracting coal from the earth. What distinguishes the definition from the reality is the horrific human costs and efforts involved in that extraction. Coal mining created the community of Centralia. It also destroyed it.

William B. Thesing, in ***Caverns of Night: Coal Mines in Art, Literature, and Film* (2000)** comes directly to the point on these costs and those efforts:

> *"Few jobs were more arduous or more dangerous than that of an underground coal miner. Hazards abounded in the 'sinister caverns' of the earth: the miners were injured or killed by cave-ins, falling rocks, accidental explosions, drownings, and poisonous gases" (2000: XI).*

In the case of Centralia, these hazards escaped the mines, surfaced, and eliminated a community founded on the economics of coal-mining. The danger that emerged from below affected not only the miner, it encircled their families as well! Today, the community of Centralia, as a social entity, has disappeared, like the coal-mining industry itself. Yet, what ended that social life remains largely hidden from view. Centralia now serves as a metaphor for the times when "coal was king", as well as for what happened (in an exaggerated form), when the "coal boom" de-evolved into a "bust"!

> **"Have Ye leisure, comfort, calm**
>
> **Shelter, food, love's gentle balm?**
>
> **Or what is it ye buy so dear**
>
> **With your pain and with your fear?**
>
> - **Percy Bysshe Shelley**

What the residents of Centralia "bought" in the mines became the death knoll of their community......

Table of Contents

Photographs

Introduction

What happens when you come back, and the only things left are the memories? Imagine every building that you once called your "hometown" was destroyed, and now absent from presence. Imagine every family that you were "raised-up" around were asked to move away from each other. Can you? And if you can, will you want to remember.........?

The Places….and the Activities

- The Mammoth Store on North Locust Street
- Demokoski's Tap Room
- Hubert Eicher High School
- Dykes Hotel
- Centralia House
- Nearly Hotel/Saloon
- Sousa's Bar
- Jack McGinley's Hotel/Tavern
- Coddington's Gulf Station ("Gassie")………..
- skating on the old Duck Pond
- "skinny-dipping" in the "Lily"
- Sleigh-riding down "Buck's Patch"……….
- Dances held in Polcovich's and Jurgill's Halls
- The Hokey Pokey Ice Cream truck
- Roller-skating in St. Ignatius Hall
- St. Mary's Ukrainian Carolers visiting the homes at Christmas
- The Rolling Donut truck
- Swimming in the "Town Dam"

The Events

- 1749: Centralia Valley bought from Native Tribes for 500 pounds.
- 1841: Bull's Head Tavern opens. The first building on the site through 1855.
- 1908: Fire destroys an entire block on Locust Avenue
- 1917: Peak of the Anthracite coal industry.
- 1918: 10% of population dies from Spanish Influenza.
- 1923: June, July- three large fires in 11 days that level large sections of Centralia (32 homes, 5 stores, hotel, warehouse, factory, shoe store were destroyed.
- 1948: 2nd worst airline disaster in U.S. history before 1950 occurs. Rescue efforts centered in Centralia.
- 1962: The fire begins......800+ buildings; 1600 inhabitants become affected.
- 2013: Today- absent presence.........

In Centralia, there were the hillers,- the down towners-,the up towners-,the back streeters-,the swampers-, and the shanties. Sections of town were called the "Swamp" (East Center/Mahanoy Street) and "Rea's Hill" (West Park/Upper Troutwine Street).

Centralia was noted for its "block parties", be it the church, the fire company, or the social organization that sponsored it. These "block parties" were the social events of the summer season, and people came from the surrounding areas to attend.

> *"It was a habit of everyone in the summertime to sit out on their front porches and they'd all say 'hello' to me. I never worried about my safety. I never worried about not being able to get help".*

If getting help was not a problem within town among the residents, it certainly <u>was</u> a problem regarding outside help: why didn't that outside help really help put out the fire?

Photo 1: "Downtown" Centralia (2013)

Centralia was so named because it was considered the "center" of everything, of people coming together. Yet, this "coming together" created tensions between ethnic identity (English, Scotch, Welsh, Irish), religion (Protestant and Catholic), and social class (coal barons, company bosses, and immigrant coal miners). This "coming together" came together because the town rests atop one of the largest veins of anthracite in the country.....in the world (the Mammoth vein). Centralia was located in the geographical center of the Western Middle Anthracite Coal Field. There were 14 mines that opened in and around Centralia.

The riches of this landscape, this "vein" of livelihood that "pumped" life into a former wilderness, and gave birth to jobs in a new land, resulted in the destruction of what came to be the former mining patch and community of Centralia, Pennsylvania. This destruction was a man-made process, both social and physical. It led to what you see today of what remains of a once-thriving coal-mining community.

Photo 2: What Remains of "Gathering Together"

The fire that started in 1962 was <u>not</u> an unnatural process brought to the surface of reality by a curse! Mine fires were part of life in the anthracite region, akin to church picnics, "hosey" bazaars, minstrel shows, and high school football. Fire was part of "life", NOT death! This "life" goes back to Native American traditions of hunting "game" in this wilderness before the discovery of coal. And this land, this "Towamensing" ("the wild place"), was seen as "cursed" long before a Catholic priest voiced it publicly. Here was a dense wilderness of narrow, thickly-grown tree-lined valleys surrounded by steep, heavily-forested hills and mountains. The wilderness was perceived as "Saint Anthony's Wilderness" by Count von Zinzendorf (1700-1760) who gave the region that name while traveling through there with Indian agent Conrad Weiser (to meet with the chiefs of several tribes whom he sought to evangelize) in 1742. Zinzendorf, who sought to unify the German Protestants of Pennsylvania, founded the town of Bethlehem.

Photo 3: Portrait of Count Von Zinzendorf

There is no curse, but this is a "cursed" land, brought about by men, not demons. There are "ghosts" here – a past occupation of land that has resulted in a surface of absence. The causes of this absence is man-made, a result of one human error after another; one human folly compounded by still others; and an ecological exploitation that surfaces again and again. As DeKok states (2010:265):

> *"The rape of the land created conditions for the town's destruction, how human misjudgment struck the match, and how bureaucracy let the Centralia mine fire burn, unable to figure out how to stop it".*

This human misjudgment and bureaucracy is described in detail at www.sonicepoch.com/centraliaalmanac/. Some of the issues include the following:

- The mine fire began as the **"result of a poor decision to illegally burn** (trash in) **a former strip-mine turned landfill".**
- **"Along with this came division of the community and constant infighting of government agencies…."**.
- **"Fire reappeared 29 May 1962 and again in June. It was quickly realized to have spread into the mines with discovery of a large unpatched hole (15 ft. wide, several feet high) which led into old mines. While it would have been fairly cheap to excavate and extinguish at this time (a quoted $175 price), the money would have to come through the proper government channels, and this delay only allowed the fire to grow".**

The various efforts to contain the fire are described. These included:

- Trenching and flushing (1962).
- Trench two (1963).

- Trench three (1965-67).
- Fly Ash Barrier (1969).
- Trench four (1969). Fly Ash Barrier Continued (1972-77). New Trench Plan (1977).
- Super Flush Barrier (1977).

To relocate or not was a constant problem within the community of Centralia. Even though the "final" vote (1983) was in favor of re-location (345-200), those that opposed the idea formed the "Residents to Save the Borough of Centralia", with 412 signatures to do nothing about the fire that would not leave Centralia intact.

In the end, in 1992, the state decided to change from a voluntary re-location to a mandatory one, declaring eminent domain on all properties in Centralia. Essentially, all remaining residents became "squatters" in their own homes and in the town they knew all their lives.

Thomas Larkin was the president of Concerned Citizens and a Centralia mine fire activist. He was a fifth-generation Centralian who had once studied for the Catholic priesthood. He had the following to say about mismanagement and governmental bureaucracy:

> *"The government promised them they would not be forced out of their homes; that's what the government said. But, I think, Government is Government, and Government lies through its teeth. I don't trust government. And I have good reason not to. Because for years, the government lied to us in Centralia. They lied to us".*

But government and bureaucracy were not the only problems. It was the mismanagement of the landscape that also contributed. Centered in this mismanagement was the exploitation of coal in the area in and around the town of Centralia.

To the east of the town is the "Badlands". It was where the fire began. Here are located a series of old strip mine pits and waste coal piles, the "culm banks". It is an eerie place, even in daylight. In the history of Centralia, it is here, in these "badlands", where people went to die. It is here where the "ghosts" of the past haunt the present absence.

Photo 4: Walking Toward the "Badlands"

Under the town of Centralia, beside the Mammoth vein, is a huge beehive of subterranean gangways. These are entrances to the "hell" that was the "life" of the anthracite coal miner. It was also the location of a "life" after the "coal boom" had ended. Here, in the cellars of some homes, "bootleg" operations took place. It was here that some "dug" for coal after the death of the industry led to unemployment and a search for revenue. Unfortunately, this "bootleg" livelihood helped create the disaster that followed. The "bootleg" operations created routes for the gases allowing the mine fire to escape, resulting in dangerous living conditions in the homes in the community.

But the biggest mistake, the most inhumane, was the treatment of children of school age. In the winter of 1980, children at St. Ignatius Elementary, located across from the church on Locust Avenue, began to complain of headaches. Shortly afterwards, above normal levels of carbon monoxide were detected in the school. Despite the apparent evidence linking carbon monoxide to the mine fire, the information was ignored, causing school children to remain in school and continue to be exposed for a year more! On June 4, 1980, a carbon monoxide detector, installed at the school, sounded for 10 minutes, until it was unplugged!

Photo 5: St. Ignatius Elementary School

Photo 6: The Elementary School Location Today (2013)

Centralia today reveals a former coal-mining community in absence, haunted by ghosts from a difficult past, and a lasting memorial of what continues into the future. The past, present, and future unfold in a way created by early man, fire, and still earlier geology (the coal veins). It is now a place marked largely by voids and ruin, and the smoke from decades of a mistake, visualized as a painful memory of a tragedy.

In absence, the understanding of past practices and politics enables one to comprehend this contemporary visualization of the consequences of place making, and how one community can embody and narrate a distinct past and prospective future. It is this absence of contemporary presence, and the still presences of past occupations that make Centralia so unique. Centralia has become a place of now abandoned spaces uniquely becoming a vision of a social memory and national (albeit international) identity that far overshadows its once restricted placement as a typical and ordinary anthracite coal-mining town. People now view Centralia as an example par excellence of how and why some individuals remain despite loss and past injustices, amid crowded spaces where the ghosts of a past vibrant community now inhabit the ruins of a spectral "ghost town".

Centralia is an example of the present as ruin, symbolizing the fragility of any physical boundary; the disturbing presence of unfulfilled aspirations; and the material remains for a haunting awareness of what might still linger in visual absence. Does this absent presence represent an exercise of the imagination, or one that requires an archaeological excavation?

Centralia is a former community that has been "peeled-back", not be archaeological excavation, but by a man-made disaster that is still in the process of ruination. How this physical presence has been removed as a documented "institutionalized excavation" can become an important visual record of reverse stratigraphy, an "incavation" rather than an "excavation"!

Some would like to think that landscapes like Centralia , that have been the scenes of exceptional and tragic events, intrinsically create a vision that complements those tragedies. Such is the case with the vision of "Hell on Earth", etched onto old Route 61 that once led into Centralia.

The reality is that such landscapes, nor what remains physically absent, say anything in themselves, even to those who have memories of what happened after an event (such as the fire of 1962 in Centralia). Centralia is empty today, but it is still full of memories. Most of those memories are not negative, and certainly do not reflect that image of "Hell on Earth". This book is meant to address those memories, engage them, "unearth" their meaning, and sense what still remains after the event of re-locating the community of Centralia.

What follows is a series of essays about Centralia, about the life of a coal-mining town. It is about what happened here, what remains, and the legacy of this history as created in the popular imagination. The story of Centralia is also an autobiography of my early life growing-up in the coal region, and because of it, how I became interested in its past through archaeology and role-playing. Playing and imagining in the ruins of anthracite decline set the stage for a contemporary understanding of what remains of Centralia after the fire forced the abandonment of a familiar way of life. It was this very "ruin" that led me to a life of "digging-deep" into the "ghosts" of the past in ruined landscapes throughout the world.

The Chinese say that if you want to create something new, you must learn to love something old. I wanted to create something out of the ruin of the anthracite coal "bust". I want to create something out of the misdirected contemporary (and popular) vision of the former town of Centralia. In the first instance, I became an archaeologist. In the case of Centralia, I use my "archaeological imagination" (Shanks 2012) to re-structure what still remains of the past at Centralia, and what significance these ruins have in the future assessment of the former town. I hope this "exercise" in a surface archaeological "excavation" will be both fruitful in stimulating the imagination and providing a serious evaluation of what happened there, and what still remains!

The "Coal Rush" Ruins

The industrial ruins (such a quaint and odd term here in this "non-industrialized" landscape) of the "coal rush", especially the "breakers" and the "collieries", stand as symbols of something past, but which still remain "active" in their symbolism. The "culm banks", silent in their waste today, retain deposits of the residual energies of past "coal-pickers". These, and other physical remains ("tipples"), are the spectral presences that haunt the present landscape. They stand still for a past that is presently merely a trace of history, noted for its absence of "working" individuals.

Photo 7: The Anthracite Past

Fragments of former activity are quite visible, within and around these coal-mining structures. This is because what we don't see, we create in absence. The imagination is the life-blood that maintains "life" in these ruined structures. Hearts still beat here but they signify a different rhythm of life. Perhaps, some of us (like myself) love these ruins because it is a human need to be reminded of our own mortality. As an archaeologist, I don't need to "excavate" too deeply to "unearth" the dead. They are quite perceptible, scattered throughout the anthracite landscape, continuing to linger in these abandoned structures.

But what happens when people, as well as these former structures are now absent? What occurs when there is no visible presence? Do we create "ghosts" in our imagination? Do we build structures in our minds in the absence of their physical remains? What do we do when a town is completely gone? What do we hope to see in Centralia today?

Do the "ghosts" from the past still keep their vigil in abandoned places such as Centralia? What happens when a place one is particularly attached to in memory, history, and experience is gone, destroyed, and physically altered? Do we just say: "something once happened here"; "someone once lived here"? Is only history, not people, remembered? But, where did that physically-visible "here" go? Do we forget the human loss, do we lower their struggle and pain, or do we imagine something more?

A "ghost" is the manifestation of "something" more. A haunting is a "still point" from the past that is <u>still</u> occupying its place in life, not history. The anthracite ruins and their empty spaces have become a phantom portal to a bygone era. They are places where everyday people (native, immigrant, and tourist) can leave (have left) their mark on the landscape.

The "ghosts" are us and our memories. They serve a basic (albeit essential) need, here in these ruins. This need is to bear witness to an existence in some form, other than a past event. There still remains, despite the loss and the absence, a continuing legacy. That legacy is the cultural heritage that I was born into, where I now stand. It forms the substance of my writings. It is a history of these ruins, and the decay that has become the anthracite "coal bust". It is the story of the <u>people</u> of Centralia, not the ruin that remains!

The Burning Memory of Anthracite Mining

"I cannot explain the draw of the mines

to someone who has never gone underground.

The air was thick with sulfur and mold, dust was everywhere.

Not even the frequent sight of friends, coworkers, strangers

crushed and maimed deterred

those of us who never got out of the mines".

- Lou Orfanella (*Memories of a Coal Miner at his Last Moments Above Ground)*

These are the memories of coal miners. These are the memories of those who worked the mines in and around Centralia. These are the memories that survive the physical absence of Centralia.........

<u>Photo 8</u>: Working in the Mines

Do the poetic thoughts expressed above echo the memories of those that remain behind in the mines and in the ruins of **"those of us who never got out"**? Are we speaking here of just the living, or the living and the dead? Do the physical skeletons of the Anthracite coal rush (the "breakers", "tipples", the "coal patches") retain more than a bare-boned existence "entombed" there in the coal, the darkness, the dust, the culm banks, and the absence? Do any "ghosts" that linger, if they could, would they leave? Do they remain out of some loyalty to the company bosses, to the town that was once Centralia? Or, is this a loyalty to family and ethnic pride?

Those miners who worked in those coal mines were literally returning to dust, even before they were officially declared dead. That exposure to coal dust in the mines led to premature death. I know, my grandfather was a victim. More than a century later, among the descendants of those ethnic miners, another deadly agent from the mines (carbon monoxide) entered the community life of Centralia. In both cases, those who worked underneath the Centralia landscape, and those who lived above, were digging their own graves from the residuals of coal mining.

Victorian poets, such as Elizabeth Barrett Browning, Joseph Skipsey, and Thomas Llewelyn, used the genre of poetry to allow the dead to speak to the living. The voices of coal miners spoke about corporate guilt and for social responsibility. Apparently, those who fought over what to do with the Centralia mine fire (both local and state government; and some Centralia citizens) did not read these Victorian poets. If they did, they did not listen to the voices of their dead miners.

In their poems, we are "listening with" these miners, as they encounter the dark **("with trembling hearts we leave the**

upper light; and travel downwards to the realms of night"), suffer in their labors, and die, with some remaining buried there in unknown and unattended grave sites. These underground excavations led indirectly to what occurred up on the surface in a small community once known as Centralia.

<u>Photo 9:</u> The Mine Environment (Pioneer Tunnel, Ashland)

There is no authority that still remains behind to lead them out of the mines, that makes them stay in the absence of a Centralia community. This makes their continuing existence here a solitary experience they re-live alone in those underground tunnels, those "bootleg" mines, and in the spaces that was once the community of Centralia. That is a sad legacy to former monumental struggles, and there is no monument to their efforts, courage, and fortitude, except the emptiness of the "badlands". Today, nobody benefits from these coal-mining "ghosts" who continue to still work the semblance of a

Centralia "community". They now only "work" from memory. How profitable is that?

At the Pioneer Tunnel in nearby Ashland, a major Pennsylvania tourist attraction, it is said that, early in the morning before the tourists come, one can still hear miners as they walk down the gangway, a habit that may still be performed long after those original footsteps have long been absent. Does a similar peripatetic walk occur in the tunnels beneath the former town of Centralia?

I have spent time alone in the Ashland mine, waiting for the "train" of students/visitors. It was Halloween 2007, and I was waiting for a group of local students to come into the mine. I was there to entertain them with coal-mining ghost stories.

As I waited, in the quiet of the mine, I walked up and down the gangway. I did not hear footsteps, but I did see bands or strings of white and blue lights moving in the dark recesses of other mine shafts. What were they? Were they the residual energies of former miners who had worked there? I don't know "who" or "what" they were. I do know the uncertainty it created in my thoughts, even before I began a single ghost story! At that moment, I was both "entertained" and the "entertainment". I was "ghosting" my forthcoming "ghost performance" for the students!

Photo 10: Inside the Pioneer Tunnel (2013)

Photo 11: Inside the Pioneer Tunnel (2013)

Photo 12: Inside the Pioneer Tunnel (2013)

In Centralia, the specter of miners still periodically surfaces, in both sight and sound. Is the contemporary "ghost town" haunted by the presences of its past history? Are the dead, buried in the town's cemeteries, returning to mourn the loss of their town? Do they rest uneasy, knowing that the homes and businesses where they experienced life are now gone? Are they concerned that their final resting places are now threatened by fire, smoke, and "ghost hunters"? Do they rise from the graveyards, and travel outward, looking for a different place of rest? "What" and "who" are they? Are they the residual memories ("recordings") of the miner's walk from home to work, and back again? Or, are they "interactive" presences ("apparitions"), those perhaps seeking a refuge from the fire and the smoke?

There is a ghost story told here about two male figures wearing mining gear who suddenly materialize (soon disappearing) at the Odd Fellows Cemetery, near the origin of the fire (1962). There are also voices that are heard in the smoke that sound like "warnings" of potential dangers in particular spaces. There are also reports of people hearing footsteps on the stairs of some of the abandoned buildings (before they were completely destroyed) when no one was observed in the vicinity.

Do these manifestations, whatever they are, signify what still remains of a once booming "coal rush" whose time is now past? For most people living today in the surrounding area, these haunting manifestations are the ghostly reminders of what has been forgotten, not remembered about the consequences of anthracite coal mining. This is what really haunts this "mined" landscape, that and the continuing fire from "Hell"!

Gaston Bachelard, French philosopher, has said this about fire:

> ***"Fire is the ultra-living element....it rises from the depth of the substance and hides there, latent and pent-up, like hate and vengeance....it shines in paradise, it burns in Hell".***

In Centralia, once thought a "paradise" by its residents, the fire spreads in the light of a tourist day, and in the darkness of a haunted, "hellish" night. A burning question about the results of this fire is: was the zip code of 17927 revoked because nobody today wants to send mail to the location of "Hell On Earth"?

Photo 13: The Lost Zip Code

The problem is <u>not</u> the "evil" or even symbolism of fire, as representing something from "Hell"; rather, it is the "evil" that men did <u>not</u> do to contain the fire that swept through the "underscape" of Centralia and the surrounding area. According to Mann (2006), **"for more than ten thousand years, most Native American ecosystems have been dominated by fire" (2006:281).**

In the Northeast, including Pennsylvania and the site of Centralia, **"Indians always carried a deerskin pouch full of flints to set fires" (Ibid: 281).** These fires were just as important for hunting game as were bows and arrows. The virgin forests were prime hunting grounds for roving bands of Native Americans. The deer here were actively pursued and hunted, if Mann is correct, through the use of fire. Thus the "coal boom" that began in the 1830's did not start the alteration of the landscape of a "pristine" forest. That change began with the use of fire by the Native Americans.

Centralia has never been, since becoming a coal-mining town, the vision of how it has appeared on the surface of the landscape. Beneath the façade of occupied buildings, there was a labyrinthian system of abandoned mine shafts, the work of ethnic miners for over 100 years, most of whom are now buried close to where they once toiled on a daily basis. That subterranean world was the "route" cause that led to the abandonment of the town and its "ruined" nature today.

The fire that continues to rage below the earth was not a "Hell on Earth". It is a "European Ghosting" (caused by the mining operations) of similar economic actions that were earlier practiced by Native Americans hundreds of years before in their hunting of game. They are human (not "demonic") actions that reflect a symmetry of actions with regard to the exploitation of this landscape. The fire that destroyed the town and landscape of Centralia must be viewed in this historical perspective. The physical destruction of occupation and exploitation, characteristic of this region for hundreds of years, has unfolded (enfolded) time and caused multiple layers of haunting uncertainties to be recorded onto this oft-mined landscape!

The Centralia mine fire and disaster is really the "tale of two worlds: the forest above, and the coal beneath. It is an integral part of Centralia's history, and its rise and fall as a coal-mining community. In the immortal and "fiery" prose of Charles Dickens:

> *"It was the best of times. It was the worst of times. It was the age of wisdom. It was the age of foolishness….It was the season of Light. It was the season of Darkness. It was the spring of hope; it was the winter of despair. We have everything*

before us, we have nothing before us....In short, the period was so far like the present period, that some of its noisiest authorities insisted on its being received, for good or for evil, in the superlative degree of comparison only" (A Tale of Two Cities).

In the tale and world of Centralia, fire was an integral element that existed in both these worlds. It became the spreading flame that would haunt the town, continuing to ignite, until nothing or no one remained, except for the ghostly memories of the past.

The role of fire existed before the coal fire. This past role of fire controlled the ecological balance of flora and fauna in the region. The Europeanization of the landscape is what caused this ecological balance to become unsettling. It is not fire that has destroyed Centralia. It was the concentrated settlement of a place that was called "Centralia", and that search for the "black diamond", that turned a natural process of ecological change into a human tragedy! It was <u>also</u> the unique characteristics of the anthracite coal. Anthracite burns very slowly, releases very little smoke, and remains combustible with little or no human intervention. Man and nature are responsible for the disaster, not the fire!

Yet, gazing at that fire that "burned" Centralia, I can see a strange and fascinating pattern emerge. This pattern is a projection of past work and activity. It has led to this land becoming devoid of human habitation, returning it once again to its "pristine" condition. But the truth of this revelation is hidden underground. This earth, beneath Centralia, is not "virgin" earth! It is "pregnant" with shafts, tunnels, and "bootleg" penetrations from the practices, passions, <u>and</u>

necessities of man (woman and child). The fire merely became the medium of transporting the ecological disaster. We can look at this fire and see something else. But is that "something" merely a repeating past, or the true significance of what remains in Centralia today?

What is wrong when nature merely followed the past ways (and contemporary abuses) of man? Understanding this tragedy is contained in the source and its "excavation". Like an ancient Native American campfire setting in those once pristine woods, the fire has itself become a storyteller. The nature of coal mining and human passion (albeit greed) has led to a disaster that came from below and was spread by <u>surface</u> mistakes!

The coal that brought warmth, and with it power and wealth became (like Native American hunts) a theatrical production. The uncontrolled spread of the flames of fire, however, have replaced the security of the "hunt", and have led to the shifting images of disaster, as the tragedy of the story of Centralia has unfolded. Fire does not kindle the same result every time it manifests. An original agent for acquiring a food source (in pre-industrial America) has become an agent for economic and social catastrophe.

When I left the coal region, where I was born and raised, to continue my education, the town of Centralia was still a functioning community (1969), even though it was surrounded by the "Badlands" of former ethnic mining operations. When I returned in 1992, the town was gone, lost to smoke, fire, and toxic fumes. In the course of my absence, Centralia disappeared! This archaeological irony is not wasted, nor is the nature of the town's ruin. But it became a ruin long before I left. The fire merely accelerated the process of (eventual) decay in this decaying anthracite landscape. Today, the populations in the cemeteries far outnumber those who continue to live in Centralia. There were once 5 hotels, 7 churches, 19 general stores, 2 jewelry shops, and 26 saloons. These are "typical" numbers in the coal region, with the saloons and bars far outnumbering the churches and other business establishments.

There is no mine fire in Mahanoy City (about 12 miles from Centralia), where I lived as a boy and where I returned at middle age (though I have since moved out of the area). Yet, Mahanoy City is just as much a "ghost town" as Centralia is. Today, there is only one functioning Catholic Church, and businesses are few (and not growing). Fire is a frequent occurrence in this town of endless row homes. The "ghosts" congregate near the rest of the "spirits", in the numerous local bars, which are ever changing and on the increase. The "end" is perhaps near because there is <u>no</u> "fire" left to excite people to action. Ruin and decay are acceptable words here because most people don't care!

Photo 14: The "Ruins" of Mahanoy City

Photo 15: The "Ruins" of Mahanoy City

Near the road that both leads into (and out) of what was (is) Centralia are two cemeteries: St. Ignatius (Catholic) and Odd

Fellows (Protestant). The gates at the St. Ignatius Cemetery are unlocked every morning and locked again at night. In what is left of Centralia, both the living and the dead are telling the rest of us something about the nature of life and death in the coal region.

Here, at Centralia, the "haunting" is a huge vertical shaft of uncertainties, containing earth, coal, air, flame, and fire. They rise, heaven-bound, though they originate deep within the earth. That "deepness" is compressed today: what lies beneath and what surfaces is slowly coming together in Centralia. Underground, the fire continues to burn along the coal seams, and the excavated spaces created by the hands of man.

On the surface, the burning below builds a toxic surface environment inhabited by spectral presences and absent structures. Above this ruined landscape, pyrocumulus clouds form. They appear as burial mounds atop the plumes of smoke rising from the fires below. They symbolize, as they float carefree above the decay, a life that has ceased to exist. That life all "went up in smoke" and formed these foreboding symbols of ruin. Halfway between heaven and "hell", the clouds that hover over Centralia are the perfect iconic symbols for separating the original plan for exploiting this wilderness (the Native American) and one too exploitative response (the coal-mining).

Centralia is part of the coal region "Badlands", a setting of old stripping holes, culm banks, and abandoned landscape dinosaurs (collieries, breakers, bootleg mine shafts, fragmented tipples, and culm banks).It is a place where I grew-up, and which sparked my archaeological imagination. It is a place that has lived and died with the rise and decline of the "coal rush".

Today, the place of Centralia, aided by an ancient element, has rushed to oblivion in an area known as the "Badlands":

"Badlands you gotta live it every day

Let the broken hearts stand

As the price you've gotta pay

We'll keep pushin til it's understood

And these badlands start treating us good.

Workin in the field till you get your back burned

Workin neath the wheels till you get your facts learned

Baby I got my facts learned real good now....

- **Lyrics by Bruce Springsteen**

Today, Centralia is as haunted as the Valley of the Kings in Egypt. It is a desolate place. Nobody goes there, except those who hope to unearth the memories of the past, or the frivolity of the present. Mine shafts and corridors, etched out of the rock by man, like the pharaoh's tombs, dot the landscape underground, buried beneath the "shifting sands" of time. The remains of the dead, killed and entombed in various episodes of mining operations, remained undiscovered. There are, however, no archaeologists willing to unearth these "coal tombs". This mining country is perfectly compatible with sites of untold remains.

This landscape that most possessed my imagination as a youth neither gave me, in the long run, suitable stimulus nor provided a home for my archaeological nature. I learned that, even in the short period of time that is a life, many things are lost that will never be recovered.

Centralia, in the span of my lifetime, illustrates quite effectively the rise and fall of an "Empire", the "Empire of Coal". These past and present moments of a personal life cannot be placed in the context of epochs. But in the end, which is not quite finished yet, I have seen and experienced firsthand what many archaeologists only uncover during a lifetime in the field. I "lived" the reality. I did not merely unearth its remains.

These "badlands" of coal country, situated between "vein" and wood, between fire and water, dealing with life and death, and among human and "ghost" is where one sees most clearly the struggle to live, survive, and grow. It has been (and is) a place where survival strategies are most wanted and needed. Here are endless opportunities and temptations to just give in and abandon one's identity. One must adapt or fall prey to ruin.

The powerful imagery of home, quite elegantly expressed in those individuals who remain in Centralia, runs deep, even deeper than the mine shafts that radiate in all directions under this "Badlands". People survive. The "ghosts" certainly do! Some remain despite the odds and dangers. They live amid the undertone of now dead and defunct activity.

But something still lingers beyond the smoke and the fire. It is something that will not go away. It is that same human spirit that first ventured here, that first settled this land, and that still remains. All these "remains" encompass that same struggle that once mined the depths of this landscape. It remains, etched onto the landscape, a part of Centralia forever. That character penetrates the void of time, the absence through death and abandonment. Those that left, and those who remain become

"a shadow among shadows brooding over the fate of other shadows that....summon up out of the all-pervading dusk" (Loren Eiseley – *"Autumn-A Memory"*).

In this coal-mining region, dusk is not confined to certain hours of the day. In Centralia, it becomes an all-day affair. The "haunted theatre" that is Centralia is burning still. When that fire will be extinguished, and another role enacted, is still a future uncertainty. It awaits someone to light a match and illuminate the way out of the mine fields.

The Multiple Layers of a Contemporary-Absent Coal-Mining Community

"The terrible gift that the dead make to the living is that of sight, which is to say foreknowledge; in return, they demand memory, which is to say acknowledgement"

- **L. Sante, *Evidence* (1992)**

Christopher Tilly, in *Metaphor and Material Culture* (1999), recognized that landscape has the potential to go beyond a visual perspective toward various imagined ones. This is a vision of "scape", a documentation of presence and remains, in the same spaces of a landscape, but using other sensory modalities. Site biographies may be incremental (like layers of strata), as the vision of "what is" moves between different social contexts.

This process of changing social contexts applies equally to ruin (as a "dead" community= an archaeological culture) as it does to a still living but declining one (present-day Centralia). These social contexts in Centralia's history include the identification of space as:

- The emerging domestic community ("coal patch")

Photo 16: Early Centralia

- The fully-developed coal-mining town

Photo 17: **The Development of a Community**

- The beginning of a landscape of ruin

Photo 18: **The Beginning of the End**

- the "ghost town"

Photo 19: The "Ghost Town"

- The haunting landscape (what physically remains from past occupations)

Photo 20: What Little Remains

These social contexts are a series of problematic visualizations that reference people (size of occupation), space (physical appearance), occupation (function), activity (purpose), and perception (experience). This results in a contemporary bricolage of identities for Centralia today that reference the same space of Centralia, as a history of occupation, has become a synecdochic community. In the increasing of absence, meanings expand. As Michel DeCerteau writes:

"What appears designates what is no more....(what) can no longer be seen".

In Centralia, the unseen (the underground fire along the coal veins) accounts for (and is the cause of) all that remains present today.

Similar forms of material culture can communicate multiple, different, and contextually diverse identities. Archaeologically, with depleted physical presence, Centralia becomes a "hauntscape" of past unseen presences. Does this create a "heritagescape" of a former coal-mining community in "boom", or a "ghostly townscape" in "bust"? There are so many possibilities that have been etched onto the contemporary landscape of Centralia:

<u>Photo 21:</u> Old Route 61: "Hell on Earth"

Photo 22: **Old Route 61: "Silent Hill"**

Photo 23: Old Route 61: "Highway to Hell"

All connotations on the "old" route "upward" toward Centralia reflect the horror of what occurred "downward" in those mine shafts: the "hell" of coal-mining. The consequences of all that coal-mining has changed the image of "downtown" Centralia from a landscape of occupation:

<u>Photo 24:</u> Centralia Before the Fire

Into an ("e")scape" of abandonment:

Photo 25: **"Downtown" Centralia, 2013**

Today, the physical "scape" of Centralia is perceived to have many guises, depending on "who" is viewing it, and what their motives are. The "scape" of Centralia is viewed as a polysemy, a biographical process of Centralia's identity over time. This becomes a polyvant biography of time and metaphoric meanings. Yet, there is a haunting presence here that has increasingly become a visual reminder that the forces of history (the coal mining enterprise), and the past acts of men (burning of trash in a former coal pit) create uncanny spaces whose contemporary meaning is constantly being transformed, each epic change displacing already embedded "ghosts" of former structures and functional spaces.

Do the perceived appearances of "ghost miners", seen through the smoke at Odd Fellows Cemetery, near the origin of the disaster, beget a kind of vengeful nostalgia: a return to an <u>unfulfilled</u> past? Does each encounter with the past become a potentially haunting one? Is what remains symbolic of something uncompleted, leaving one with feelings of guilt for having explored it? How does the presence of what remains contribute to coal-mining heritage?

The ruined landscape that is now Centralia is an example of our obligation to the future, before the histories, the eyewitnesses, and the testimonials are lost and forgotten. This acknowledgement must become the legacy of memory work in (and about) Centralia. This is a lesson we must learn through constructive fieldwork. It is a heritage that we must preserve to legitimize and memorialize those who came before, and what was lost in the process of ecological ruin.

Why do people still stay in Centralia, one may legitimately ask? Is it because they still identify with the absence as "home"? Is this nostalgia or something else? Michel de Certeau has said that **"haunted places are the only ones that people can live in" (quoted in Edensor 2005:152).** What "haunts" those who remain? Is it the plight of the immigrant, a childhood familiarity with spaces and objects in new settings? Is it the fear of exploring and re-settling in an unfamiliar space?

Do these grandsons and granddaughters of immigrants no longer listen to "the immigrant song"? Does what circulate in their blood, rather than tie them to ancestral migrations, unite them to a landscape that is similar to that underground experience of shafts, tunnels, and now abandoned, worthless space? Are they symbolically tied to the ground, as they remain "trapped" by what lies beneath their feet, and the legacy of the "coal rush" boom?

Centralia is certainly haunted by its past. But is this "haunting" a part of their heritage, their landscape, their memories, the ecological disaster, or the presence of the "ghosts" of what might have been? Do real apparitions manifest here as a result of past history and human error and tragedy? If so, are the revenants, perceived by some individuals who come here, manifestations of the guilt or culpability of human error or greed?

Has the appearance of a "ghost" become a social figure through which something lost (or forgotten) be made to re-appear again? Does the "ghost" reflect the trauma of what happened here, what's left, and how to work with what's left? Does the belief that the Centralia landscape is haunted reflect a selective remembering of particular understandings of past situations here? I don't know. I do know, however, that regarding Centralia today, the words of Alfredo Gonzales-Ruibal haunt me. Is Centralia an example of an **"empty place in a forest full of ghosts"**?

The land, once stripped bare to "raise" a town that supplied fuel for others, and the earth beneath that was hollowed-out to erase man's dreams and aspirations, has now simply begun to return to its once long forgotten earlier history of absence, in a forest full of trees. Only now, instead of the bear, deer, and mountain lion, there are the "ghosts" from multiple past occupations of human presence. Reverting back to a Native American presence and spirituality, and the use of fire, it is the way the past comes back to haunt the living, and the way that Centralia contains its pasts.

This goes beyond the visual, the physicality of the remains, or the historical documentation that transformed the community into a ghost town and "spectralscape". It goes beyond the contemporary vision of ruin as the <u>final</u> expression of human occupation – because it is not! This is the past as non-absent. It is the past as a series of haunting images and sensuous experiences:

- The past interruption of the present, transforming its future image;
- Past vision becoming present again and prompting various reactions; and a
- Reanimated past that resonates and makes sense to us today!

This is the role of the Centralia landscape today: a present-day "heritage hauntscape"! As DeCerteau describes:

> *"There is no place that is not haunted by many different spirits, hidden there in silence, spirits one can 'invoke' or not".*

In the "scape" of Centralia, they are many and varied. Here are a few of their images:

<u>Photo 26</u>: The Historical Past

<u>Photo 27</u>: The Contemporary Past

<u>Photo 28</u>: The Present

The Re-Making of Centralia

Someone once said that the past can only be dealt with when the causes of the past are removed. If contemporary vision has been characterized by absence, with causes dating back into Centralia's history, obscured by smoke and toxic fumes from the mine fire, how much more important memory becomes. As the site further de-evolves into ruin, these memories are significant non-material elements of Centralia's cultural heritage of the "coal rush boom". Let's acknowledge the memory of Centralia as it was: a vibrant ethnically-diverse, and heritage-laden, coal-mining community; and not what it has become, a vision of this "hell on earth"!

If the contemporary vision of Centralia has been associated with absence, obscured by "smoke screens", how much more is this presence of memory? Yet this memory is a manifestation that is largely "unseen" in today's popular cultural venues about Centralia. It is one that equates the fate of Centralia with the movie, "Silent Hill"(2006) , a theme, as we have seen, popularized on the "graffiti road" of old Route 61.

Silent Hill's screenwriter, Roger Avary, used Centralia as his inspiration for the town of "Silent Hill". Avary's father, a mining engineer, used to tell him stories about Centralia when he was a boy. Centralia has been used as a model for the manifestations of "Hell" in other popular works.

Dean Koontz's short novel, **Strange Highways (1995),** depicts a fictional Centralia as a wasteland full of evil people at the gates of Hell. In the introduction to the novel, he lists the Centralia mine fire as an inspiration. The book is a journey:

"into subterranean depths where the darkness of the human soul breeds in every conceivable form....over unfamiliar terrain populated by the denizens of Hell".

- www.deankoontz.com/strange-highways/

David Wellington used Centralia in his ***Vampire Zero* (2008)** as the town where vampire hunter, Laura Coxton, returns. Again, the town is depicted as "Hell":

"I know there's a Hell. I grew up with it under my feet".

In George C. Chesboro's novel, ***The Beasts of Valhalla* (1985),** the ground beneath the town of Centralia served as a secret genetic modification lab. Edward Bloor's novel, **A Plague Year (2011),** describes the town of "Caldera", which was inspired by Centralia. This is the story of a small coal-mining Pennsylvania town ("Blackwater") in the fall of 2001, when terrorists (the nearby downing of Flight 93) and methamphetamine suddenly began big threats.

Centralia is the hometown of the main character in the crime novel, ***Dirty Blonde* (2009),** by Lisa Scottoline:

"She lived in Philadelphia since law school, but her heart wasn't in the city. She'd grown up in the mountains, from a small town erased from the map".

Scottoline chose the coal-mining town of Centralia as the setting of her book because the main character, Cate, and the town had interesting similarities. Like Centralia, **"Cate has an underground mine fire of her own".** Whatever that means, I personally don't know!

The main character in Joyce Carol Oates, ***The Tattooed Girl,*** Alma Busch, whose life **"is a symphony of tragedy after**

tragedy", is from Centralia, an appropriate setting. It seems that the author's intention, according to the Pittsburgh Post-Gazelle's review (June 8, 2003) **"was to show the absolute worst outcome for females who leave the hearth"**. Was leaving Centralia really worse than staying?

Episode 200 of **"The Simpsons" ("Trash of the Titans")**, which won the Emmy for Outstanding Animated Program in 1998, was loosely based on Centralia's history. In the episode, which included U2 playing themselves, Homer becomes Springfield's Sanitation Commissioner and charges other towns to dump their trash into an abandoned mine. When the trash begins "erupting" out of the ground, the entire town is re-located.

In music, the group **"Squonk Opera"** wrote a musical entitled **"Inferno"**. This was a re-interpretation of Dante's **"Inferno"**, and it used Centralia as a trip into "Hell. The Danish musician, **Trentemoller**, used Centralia as a location for his music video, **"Sycamore Feeling"**. **"Car Bomb"**, a mathcore band from Long Island, New York, released **"Centralia" (2007)** as its first full-length album, a tribute to the town. The metal band, **"Jucifer"** wrote **"Centralia" (2006),** a song about the mine fire. Here are the lyrics:

> *"What the ground holds will be silent now*
> *And the earth scorched by the molten plough*
> *And the trees bare in the valley and*
> *All the streets clear*
> *In the Centralia.*
>
>
> *What the ground hides makes the breezes sour*
> *And the blooms wilt as the rooys devour.*

We'll be staying for our homes are here
Ever drying
And the streets are clear.

Ever drying and the trees are bare
In the valley of the shadow
In the valley
Of Centralia".

There are two other movies with Centralia in the script. The movie, **Made in USA (1987)**, starred Adrian Pasdar and Chris Penn, and was directed by Ken Friedman. This is the story of two young men who decide to leave behind their working-class lives in a Pennsylvania coal-mining town, and travel to California. Partially filmed in Centralia, it is considered **"one of the best visual records of the town as it was being evacuated"**.

However, there a number of erroneous dialogue tracts, such as the opening sequence, mouthed by Penn:

> *"Fire started in the dump....it was Good Friday so no one would leave church to put the thing out; figured they'd do it the next day..."*

This is not true, and contradicts the known facts. The box description is also not very accurate:

> *"Two coal miner sons who have given up on their town, their families and the way of life they once knew......"*

I don't think so! Most people in Centralia did not want to move. In fact, many of those who were forced to leave are "dying" to come back: plots are still being sold at St. Ignatius cemetery, and former residents, who relocated out of town, are being interred there, as it was their desire to be buried back home!

The worst movie depiction, however, of Centralia was the film, **Nothing But Trouble (1991).** It starred Chevy Chase, John Candy, and Demi Moore, and was directed by Dan Aykroyd. It was a spoof of Centralia. The movie was a dark, twisted, unfunny, and over-acted comedy!

All of these cinematic and fictional depictions of Centralia have left their mark, unfortunately, on the popular imagination. Besides the consequences of the fire, and the move away from home, the people of Centralia have to also endure these inaccurate and unflattering portraits of their town and their life.

In books and accounts about the tragedy of Centralia, there are also stories about the pedophile who raped and killed a 13 year old girl (just before the tragic fire began), and the couple who argued about whether to stay or leave Centralia (after the consequences of the fire were know). Tragically, the argument led to a murder-suicide. Both incidents occurred in the "Badlands" east of town.

But tragedy and death in Centralia have a deep history, all relative to coal-mining. Besides the loss of life due to coal-mining-related accidents, there was the violence associated with alleged Mollie Maguire activity. This included:

- The killing of Alexander Rea, Superintendent of the Locust Mountain Coal and Iron Company, who was robbed on the road between Mt. Carmel and Centralia. Rea had a large house in Centralia, and it was he who named the town and laid-out the street grid. He also donated the land for the building of St. Ignatius Catholic Church. The murder occurred on October 17, 1868.

- The ambush and hanging of Thomas Dougherty (on North Locust Avenue in Centralia) in 1874.
- The killing of Michael Lenahan, shot to death in front of his home (Locust and West Park Streets) in 1874.
- The killing of John Gunning by Edward Curley in 1876. Gunning was shot when he complained about a thin layer of huckleberries that was sold to his wife.

The people of Centralia have endured, despite all the tragedies, the death, the killings, and the ecological disaster that ended the town's existence. The landscape of Centralia has become a site of national social memory because it is a place that "burns" with embodied presences in a vision of absence. It has become a symbolization of ruin, decay, loss, cultural politics, and something deeper still. This is seen (as depicted in the photos above) along the former main thoroughfare into town, Route 61 as a "Hell on Earth". This "Hell on Earth" embodies multiple meanings:

- The fire below, the surface smell of sulphur, and the escaping toxic fumes onto the surface of the former town; and
- The "hellish" conditions of work in the underground mines.

This "hell on earth" today, and the cause of the mine fire that began in 1962 was relayed to the clean-up of the land-fill for Memorial Day: remembering the dead (and the past) indirectly created a future "dead" town! There was also the coal mining world of darkness that changed to deadly colors: glowing orange, flickering blue, and a burst of yellow when timbers ignited, after the fire spread along the old mine gangways!

The "death" of the community by fire, smoke, "colored" visuals, and toxic fumes has "buried" what was once Centralia. This has left little foundation for physical history. It has produced an archaeological cemetery of remains:

> *"Death appears to result in the paradoxical production of both disappearance and remains. Disappearance....clings to remains-absent flesh does ghost bones".*

- **Rebecca Schneider,** *Performing Remains* **(2011)**

What is left in Centralia is merely the bare "bones" of former foundations, representing homes, businesses, and other structures:

Photo 29: Foundation Remains

Photo 30: Foundation Remains

Photo 31: Foundation Remains

These foundations form a gathering place of memories that have served different functions throughout the history of Centralia, as a location of socio-cultural occupation. This is a memory of presence that is both seen (the foundations) and unseen (the coal veins and fire underneath). Each functioned to create a layer of occupation:

- Coal "patch"
- Mining community
- Ghost town; and
- Spectral "hauntscape".

This layering of strata of various functional occupations can be seen in the very space where the fire started in 1962. Here, we have successive deposits of:

- Strip mining
- Garbage dump
- Site of frequent burning of this garbage
- Site of the mine fire (1962) and

- Location of reported manifestations of spectral "coal miners".

Photo 32: The Contemporary location of the 1962 mine fire

This vision(both historical and folkloric) of "occupied" Centralia space is not so much a linear occupational history, as it is an archaeological matrix, a symmetry of common elements through time that unfold back onto itself. This is a genealogy of fire, coal mining, ethnic and religious strife, and ecological exploitation. We have ample visual and historical documentation of this "road to ruin" but we are constrained by what we can explore today due to the present inherent dangers.

The location of Centralia, on the summit of the mountain, was perceived as an idealized and privileged physical location, compared to the "coal patches" that were located along the side of the mountain. The contemporary scene of Centralia, however, is perceived as worse than its movie ("Silent Hill") counterpart. It has become an empty place full of the "ghosts" of the past <u>and</u> the "phantom" presences who come here to witness "death" and leave their "marks" in the often callous graffiti on old Route 61.

Photo 33: "Graffiti Road"

We must alter this view of Centralia as this spectral landscape, a "Hell on Earth". We must compose a different Centralia tune, seeking a melody linked to cultural and social expressions of the Anthracite community. This would engage us with acts of remembrance that work to create ways to recognize Centralia's past, while engaging its future vision of heritage management:

> *"They volunteered their spare time at the church and the fire department, sipped draft beers at the*

> ***Legion, and tended to elderly relatives and neighbors. They had a respect for family, place, stability, and tradition....***" (Quigley 2007:158).

A contemporary perspective with links to the past is a geo-ethnographic approach which means to take ghosts seriously! This focus on "ghosts" is not so much about a phantom presence, or a scary story (though what happened here does haunt us), as it is about what did not occur here.

Fire, coal mining, politics, and ecological manipulation only haunt Centralia in the wrong way. This wrong way has caused, in large measure, its present display of physical and human absence. Whether one believes in ghosts or not, these ghosts of the past must be confronted! It is a personal choice whether one invokes them or not. But it must be understood that a "haunting" is an important concept because **"to haunt is to possess some place" (Steve Pile).**

Henri Lefebvre, in *The Production of Space* (1992) says that **"no space ever vanishes utterly, leaving no trace".** At Centralia, the remains of "ghosts", as traces and vestiges of remains in space and history, are a <u>good</u> thing. Those who still remain there in 2013 know this is certain. And that is why they have not left!

The dangers of coal mining created a "band of brothers". Ben Rush, a geography professor, quoted in DeKok (2010) has said:

> **"A tiny universe of experience....highly dependent on who they know....a life built on a sense of social ties. You take that away and there's nothing (2010:16).**

In this part of Pennsylvania, a move-even a short one-created tensions:

- Different ethnic mixes
- Different religions
- Different social attitudes.

In the minds of these "home bodies" who didn't want to move, Centralia was the **"Brigadoon of the Anthracite Region" (DeKok 2010:204).** That is why those who remain stay in "Centralia". Perhaps, it is also why the "ghosts" of the past remain too? Evacuation was not an option for many (for many a year after the fire started). Their homes were their "pride and joy", perhaps creating what famous ghost hunter Hans Holzer had called the **"stay-behinds"** (those who loved their home and community so much that they "stayed-behind" after death). Who knows?

The Ghosts of Place: The Archaeological Perspective

Individuals invoke ghosts when they identify the ruin that is now Centralia as culturally significant (popular culture through film), mark a now largely deserted landscape as historic, or visit spaces of Centralia memory through tours. People have re-made Centralia without physically constructing a building. They do this through moments of memory of past experience that create new haunting spaces, and re-mediate former social spaces.

This place-making into a haunted Centralia identifies defunct social arenas as ghostly where they, and their memories, can return, or where the ghosts of the past saunter forward from mine shafts, past symbolically through the cemetery, and out toward South Locust Street. It is not at all surprising that "ghost miners" appear near where the original fire began, in a dump near the Odd Fellows Cemetery. This becomes a blend of history, folklore, and memory traces of past presence.

Photo 34: The Odd Fellows Cemetery

The dump-cemetery complex marks a contemporary haunted social space where people and ghost make contact with their loss, restrict unwanted presences from the past, and identify where perceived past injustices are located and contained. It is here where emotions and relations with the past are constructed and become "unearthed".

Centralia has become a place of social memory for more than its former inhabitants, or those who still remain in its community spaces. This is because it is a space that burns with embodied presences in a vision of absence and the symbolization of ruin, decay, and something deeper still than mere absence.

This vision of embodied presence has become visualized in the former thoroughfare through town, old Route 61, now labeled a "Hell on Earth", with cracks and fissures exposing the hell-like and horrific conditions of what it once meant to work underground in the coal shafts that are located underneath the town and the former roadway. It is the heat of overwork that burns through the exposed road surfaces that symbolizes what it was like to live and work underground.

Photo 35: The Fire "Unearthed" on old Route 61

Photo 36: Another Example

Some say a curse was put on the town by a Catholic priest. This is the text of that "curse":

"You will all pay for your support of those murderers, the Molly Maguires. I place a curse on all those that are responsible for this crime (beaten after refusing to stop preaching against the violence attributed to the Mollies), **on their families and on their children. One day this town will be erased from the face of the earth.....".**

<u>Photo 37</u>: Father Daniel J. McDermott

Father Daniel J. McDermott, who spoke those words, was the founding priest of St. Ignatius Church (1869). St. Ignatius, constructed of native rock gathered from the mountain, was the oldest Catholic Church in the region. Father McDermott's middle name was Ignatius. The root of "Ignatius" is the Latin "ignis", meaning "fire", an interesting relation to the "curse" and what occurred later (the "fire").

Father McDermott was known for his anti-Molly Maguire stance, and his aggressiveness in the crusade against this organization. He became well-known throughout the Catholic Church in the United States for this crusade. He was eventually reassigned to another church for his own safety. But in 1876, he spiritually "prepared" the six condemned "Mollies" in Pottsville, Pennsylvania before they were hanged on the "Day of the Rope" (June 25, 1876). It is reported that he wrote a personal account of the "Mollies", but his friends advised against publishing it. It lay in the drawer of his desk in the study at the rectory. It is said that, shortly before his death, he burned it.

Though his "cursed" words echoed what occurred in Centralia more than a century later, it was no "curse" that caused the fire. Its origin was socio-political, a product of the coal barons and their exploitation of the mammoth coal vein. And the spark that ignited it came from the negligence of man. And those "cursed", the former ethnic miners, are largely gone, or are they? Do they return, as some have reported?

Photo 38: St. Ignatius Catholic Church, Centralia

Photo .39: The Interior of St. Ignatius Church (before its demolition)

Photo 40: The Demolition of St. Ignatius

If a community is characterized by a body of diverse work and social acts, why are their "ghosts" perceived simply as "coal miners"? Is this a remembrance of something important, a symbolism of what occurred here, such as social injustice? Did this injustice begin with the "curse" of Father McDermott toward a certain group of ethnic coal miners?

What remains of Centralia, and the legacy of coal mining here, has become a particular haunted archaeology, layers of memory that have created a post-occupational meaning from the ruin of physical presence, as time and social identity have marked this landscape. No "digging" is involved to "unearth" these "ghosts". These elements make their own presences known on the surface today, disguised in many forms. Past, present, and future are understood in Centralia as co-constitutive!

From an archaeological perspective, particular core concepts come into focus in Centralia, and should be countered by investigative forensic fieldwork. These core concepts include:

- "Being"
- "Presence"
- "Forms of (Cultural) Life".

The philosopher, Heidegger (1971) has remarked:

> *"being now no longer means what something is. We hear 'being' as a verb, as in 'being present', and 'being absent'; means it persists in its presence" (1971:95).*

Centralia is a haunted location where research must change from a "ghost hunt" for a "being" as a "life form" to something becoming present as a form of (former) life. Fieldwork must become an excavation of what and who remains from the past. The "ghost" becomes a form of life that persists in its presence, despite the absence of most physical remains of what was once a vibrant coal-mining community. To do this, we must look beyond the absence toward the presences that still remain <u>and</u> the memory of those who knew Centralia as it was!

The Centralia question, relative to a landscape (or "hauntscape") of public knowledge centers on the study of its past as a form of heritage. The archaeological question is this: to what extent is Centralia, with its contemporary absence of visible presence and embodied remains, worthy of consideration as this "heritage" of coal-mining? The answer lies in the attitude and behavior of those individuals who go there: do they envision the absence as something still present; can they "read" what still remains? That response will be what haunts Centralia's future, and may help to transform its present state of absence and ruin.

These future transformations become a new layering of certainty. But how do we document these transformations?

- Do we conduct an archaeological survey that documents de-composition, rather than an excavation of site formation?
- Do we merely record this visual destruction, rather than develop a virtual re-construction?
- Do we use a field strategy in the use of the "archaeological imagination"?
- Do we take a stance as a "witness" to a former past becoming present again?

These are questions of significance and deep meaning. And it is a means to externalize the symbolism of a place such as Centralia, its history, and recognizing its multiple meanings. This is to identify the context in which the site functioned as a particular social entity. It is the social significance of Centralia in its temporal and cultural context.

An Alternative Approach to What Remains of Centralia

"Mining is a community of occupation, not a community of place...."

- **Municipal Judge Neil V. Reynolds, a Fifth-Generation resident of Leadville, Colorado.**

Mining communities, the normative view (at least for the mining of metals, such as Leadville), are most likely to be conceived as ephemeral locations, created by individuals who saw residence as both temporary and transitory. This type of "community" leaves little trace in the material record, even for archaeologists.

Is this the same situation for the mining of coal? Certainly, many of the historic "coal patches" attached to former mining operations are now gone, particularly in adjacent Schuylkill County, Pennsylvania. Centralia is typical of a mining community in that it is representative of a domestic space of people who were heterogeneous in character (diverse ethnic backgrounds/origins), and who were brought together by the need to work.

The town of Centralia, however, has proven that the perception of the ephemerality of metal-mining communities, both as to its transitory nature and the remains that are left after the event (re-location) is not applicable there. Centralia is no temporary location in the hearts and minds of those who once lived there. Centralia remains "home" for many: some remain, and some return.

One of our deepest needs as humans is a sense of identity and belonging. A common theme in this need is an attachment to a particular landscape, and how those who sense that attachment find identity. A landscape is defined by our vision of it, interpreted by our minds with a little help from imagination.

How does one maintain that vision in the presence of absence in that landscape today? Do the people who once lived and worked in Centralia feel that sense of identity and belonging still? Certainly their vision of their community is not one popularly portrayed as "Hell on Earth"! Nor is that vision a certain one of absence, decay, and ruin.

A landscape can be seen as a cultural construct in which the sense of a place is a continuing process of populating that landscape. This certainly has occurred in Centralia, as the notion of that landscape has changed from a coal-mining community to multiple (and popular) images in books, movies, song, and social media. Landscapes, therefore, are shaped by mental attitudes. A proper understanding of landscape must rest then on the historical recovery of what remains <u>after</u> the event. In the case of Centralia, this "event" is the re-location of its community, and the demolition of its community structures.

This "recovery" is usually the focus of archaeology. In the field, archaeologists ask many questions in their exploration of a site. One of these questions, particularly appropriate for the Centralia landscape is this: How do we sense and document the past, that which remains after an event, as past acts of behavior?

How do our senses work across time, or do they? How do we "recover" that sense of Centralia's identity, and the sense of the community which once belonged here, in the midst of absence and ruin? Does the past remain present today in Centralia? If it does, how do we sensibly approach that past presence <u>without</u>

altering that sense of identity and belonging (and remain true to the historical record of the Centralia community)?

> ***"Excavation has a unique role to play as a theatre where people may be able to produce their own pasts which are meaningful to them, not as expressions of a mythical heritage".***

- **C. Tilley, "Excavation as Theatre" (1989).**

Centralia is no mythic "Hell on Earth". It was, and still is, a coal-mining community in the memory of many of its former residents. Through an archaeological sensitivity and sensibility, and with the "voices" of its former residents, we can make this empty site a space of contemporary cultural production. We can give Centralia a different contemporary vision, where other times, norms, social interactions, and cultural rules are <u>still</u> in operation.

One means to accomplish this is through site-specific performances, and the use of contextual sounds (as "triggers"), ones that would be familiar to Centralia as a coal-mining community. There is nothing special (or innovative) about "staging" a "theatrical" performance at an archaeological site (cf. Pearson and Shanks 2001). However, site-specific performances are different:

> ***"A large part of the work has to do with researching a place, often an usual one that is imbued with history or permeated with atmosphere" (Pavis 1998:337).***

Centralia is a perfect location for a site-specific performance. Though Centralia was never a "ghost town", it went directly, however, to being a "ghostly" landscape. Yet, the poetics of abandoned landscapes can inform us about experiencing them. They allow us to recover personal dramas (Buchli and Lucas 2001), and memories of a time and place before tragedy struck.

Walking the now abandoned streets, interrupted by the occasional sidewalk and entrance to a former residence, a chance encounter with a discarded household object (or a broken toy) can convey a variety of emotions and can haunt us with a past that is no more.

Photo 41: An Abandoned Centralia Sidewalk

These now "useless" disregards become valuable artifacts. They convey a message, both warning us and cautioning us. These become little "monuments" to a past that remains reachable, even when vision suggests nothing much remains. One must be cautious so as not to link absence with total loss or forgetfulness, when there is still memory. We must refrain from imagining the "other" when these remains suggest familiarity.

The ruin that is Centralia has too often been portrayed in a negative way. While it is sad to see a town "die", it is sadder still to forget those memories, to deny they remain, and to erase a community by constructing something "other". By "burying" the memories, the whole Centralia occupation is exorcised!

When we sense the past of Centralia, do certain senses predominate in different historical periods in the same physical space? For example, during the American Civil War, in the "culture of war", the sense of sound was important, especially on a battlefield, where visual acuity was curtailed.

Are their hierarchies of value within a particular sense? Within a sound sense, for example, the occurrence of particular "soundmarks" becomes important. Soundmarks are particular sounds that are "markers" characteristic of a particular community. In Centralia, many of these soundmarks would be relative to coal mining.

A community of soundmarks creates a soundscape, rather than a physical landscape. Since most physical features are now absent in Centralia, a logical research thrust would involve an analysis of the contemporary Centralia soundscape.

Because of the importance of sound in some cases, observation is not a final judgment of interpretation. It becomes merely one field method. Vision is not simply (or only) the source of enlightenment, evaluation, or science. Vision certainly cannot be used <u>exclusively</u> in Centralia today to ascertain what remains after the event of re-location has ended the community's existence. But is the physical death of the town really an end to the community of Centralia? I think not.

There is still the soundscape of Centralia. Soundscapes have a spatio-temporal component that "lift-up over" the sounds of contemporary space. They also have "soundings" that attach themselves to particular historical periods (such as the "soundmarks"). A soundscape helps to define physical space, even when that space is void of physical structures.

A soundscape also communicates social interaction and flow. It defines boundaries and personal space, and engages individuals in multiple ways. Sound is not only eventful. It is part of everyday life, especially in pre-industrial (and pre-hyperlink) societies where long-distance communication was made by these soundmarks, not cell phones and the internet.

Does the soundscape of Centralia, however, still "speak" to us today, even in its ruined and fragmented state? Can we have a "conversation", a dialogue, a communicative performance within its physical spaces? A landscape unfolds through how people move in and through it, going about their daily routines. Many of these daily routines at Centralia were enacted by, and performed to, particular sounds. How much of this survives after the event of re-location?

I am an archaeologist. I deal with the sites of the dead, with those in ruin and decay. I do not deal with the sites of the living. I treat these sites with upmost respect, and not as forms of "entertainment". I am very careful NEVER to "pollute" or "contaminate" these sites with objects or behaviors from my own time, to avoid confusing archaeologists in the future. This is my cardinal rule when working in the field.

Centralia should be viewed as an <u>interactional</u> community created through relationships and associations. These relations and associations conserve the sense of community, even when the physicality in which it is based (the town, homes, and businesses) is no longer in existence. This interaction and association can be perceived in the way former residents talk about their life here, and also when the "dead" return to be interred in the local cemetery (such as St. Ignatius).

This view of a <u>continuing</u> community of Centralia in physical absentia is what distinguishes Centralia far and above its popular associations in social media. Centralia, as a community, continues to be more than the sum of its now loose, disconnected parts!

It is this approach, not its various popular renditions described above, that one must approach a Centralia of the future, even as its human landscape (the physicality of residence) continues to decay and expand into more ruin and trace elements.

An important question is this: "What is the Centralia community, in the presence of absence, today?" is an important research endeavor. Can Centralia, its past presence, still be considered a relatively static, conservative, closed, and homogeneous community that continues a shared normative culture of experiences that were common to its inhabitants? The answering of these two questions is how we are approaching our research into contemporary Centralia.

This research involves a socio-spatial patterning that is based on a social recognition and a self-recall of this patterning. This view of a "normative" community appears to be compatible with the unit of archaeological analysis called the "site". It includes several archaeologically-visible material "markers", and still others requiring the use of the "archaeological imagination" (Shanks 2012). These visible material "markers" include:

- Discrete spatial patterning of activities (cemeteries, "dump" site, baseball field, the former residential space of Alexander Rea, etc.).
- Residential nucleation (various house foundations along former streets).
- Shared material culture (remains of the efforts to combat the fire; residuals of the continuing underground fire).

These interactional "markers" remain structured and synchronized by a set of places/spaces contained within a particular span of time (and correspond to various periods in the history of Centralia).

Besides these material "markers", there are other more ephemeral elements within the landscape (or "hauntscape"). These include particular "soundmarks" that identify this landscape as a coal-mining community, and as the town of Centralia within this anthracite region. Soundmarks are unique sounds that characterize a particular community.

This non-ocularcentric approach to landscape is especially suited for Centralia where the absence of people and physical structures is now the norm. A reliance on sound rather than sight is a form of sonic geography, and is part of acoustic archaeology. The recording of the contemporary soundscape, with "roots" going back into Centralia's past, is used in our investigative analysis to separate the historical Centralia from an "imagined" Centralia, as popularized in fiction, music, cinema, and the tropes of popular "ghost hunting".

This approach is an attempt to "unearth" the remaining "aural culture" of Centralia, and one of its most compelling aspects: its emphasis on listening to <u>other</u> voices, those that are <u>not</u> visibly present:

> *"Now I will do nothing but listen*
>
> *To accrue what I hear into this song, to let sounds contribute toward it....*
>
> *I hear all sounds running together, combined, fused or following*
>
> *Sounds of the city, and sounds out of the city, sounds of the day and night".*

- **Walt Whitman, *'Song of Myself'***

Today, amid the ruin, is Centralia silent? In the presence of absence, do they still "make a sound" in Centralia? Are there sounds of human voices at work, play, and performing habitual acts (such as walking)? We have come here to find out.

In this age of instant communication and the cell phone, it is an opportunity (in Centralia) to locate and advocate for a fieldwork agenda where a slower pace of life occurred. Centralia, today, is a place (and a landscape) where one can develop a capacity to listen sensitively, rather than over-hear!

The concept of the recognition of "soundmarks" as "signals", and verbal dialogue as "agents" for contextual response recordings are important considerations in our fieldwork at Centralia. Recognition and recall form the operational process (and analysis) for the auditory data that we record in our investigations.

This research, and its operational acts in the field, is, at the present time within the Centralia landscape, in its infancy. In our research, we advocate a consideration of Centralia as a continuing community of presences, a dynamic socially-interactive and constituted process of communication that is contingent upon outside human agency for its manifestation and continued existence.

This community of Centralia, as a continuing presence in the absence of a structured physicality, is defined not just by spaces, individuals, and acts. It is, more importantly, identified by historical context. It is these elements (space, individuals, and acts in particular histories) which define our auditory remains of a continuing Centralia community.

Though this is the beginning of an auditory archaeology of a contemporary Centralia soundscape, and its continuing sense of community, some preliminary results can be discussed here. Our preliminary soundscape survey of Centralia began in April, 2013. Another soundscape survey will be conducted in late July 2013.

Photo 42: A Peripatetic Walk through the Centralia Landscape

Photo 43: Recording the Centralia Soundscape

Based on our preliminary soundscape survey in Centralia, we have recorded a number of sounds that are contextual to a life in Centralia before the consequences of the underground fire forced the re-location of the community. We have not yet determined whether these sounds are relative to the period before the fire (1962), or occurred afterwards.

We are returning in late July 2013 to conduct more contextual acoustical studies in order to locate and place these sounds within a particular time frame of the Centralia soundscape. We approach what remains of the Centralia community and its soundscape as a social interactional process, and not an historical "text", simply to be "read" onto what remains (such as the "Hell on Earth" motif, or the absence of presence signifying a complete loss of the remains of the Centralia community).

In the context of a "sound" analysis, the making of a social exchange can be enacted. A place, largely abandoned like Centralia, is re-generated by the situation of the use of auditory soundmarks. Their use becomes a moment, a field of interaction, opened by auditory knowledge. It makes no difference what physically remains. It makes all the difference what is sounding out.

From this perspective, a soundmark locates us within an animate and energetic environment, not a "dead zone". This animated environment often exceeds the conventional ranges and possibilities of representation. Absence becomes presence. Sound disregards the visual and the material presence, displacing and replacing them, making it a perfect complement for what is left in place in a space once called Centralia.

The acoustic space that opens creates a time. It is not bounded in time, as an element that is past and buried (or forgotten). The use of soundmarks brings a past back from the depths of history into the present. In traveling away from its origin, sound becomes current, as it is carried forward (brought back) through memories and recordings. The soundmark explicitly brings times and events together, even in the absence of physical remains.

A landscape has ontological significance. Since Centralia (or what's left of it) has been lived in, it remains replete with meanings, not just something looked at, or thought about (and imagined). Centralia, even today, is some place much more than a place of absence. As an archaeologist, use to "digging-deeper" into the meaning of place, I examined Centralia through the analysis of remembering and forgetting those moments of living there.

We came to Centralia in April of 2013 in order to conduct an analysis of the landscape's sounds (its present and past soundscape). Besides the contemporary sounds of activity, we also recorded the sounds of past presence. These were recorded during contextual performances that were acts relative to various activities in Centralia's past. They were focused on children's activities: games and local places that would have been part of growing-up in Centralia prior to the fire of 1962.

We are returning again in late July 2013 to continue our soundscape survey of Centralia. Both of these surveys are background research before conducting a full-scale site-specific performance (see below) at Centralia sometime in the spring of 2014. We believe that a site-specific performance of Centralia's past would help to eradicate the current negative image of this landscape as one of absence and abandonment.

Rather than portray Centralia as a landscape of ruin and absence (or worse a "Hell on Earth"), we would use this ruin and absence as a form of emplacement for our site-specific performance. Our site-specific performance would, as Tilley suggests, re-imagine Centralia as a space of continuing shared social interactions, creativity, and cultural expressions of the community's past with those who once lived there, and those whose memories of an occupied Centralia have not been lost and forgotten.

The site-specific performance is meant to "unearth" the memories of Centralia before it was abandoned. The co-sharing of this event by participants, observers, and the "ghosts of place" will create a renewed landscape where past memories are recognized and recalled, and a new form of remembrance is generated. The site-specific performance, as a mode of contemporary cultural production, will allow us to **"take up the fragments of the past and make something out of them in the present...." (Pearson 2010:48).** This will allow a more favorable future image of Centralia to be generated.

A Future for Centralia:

The Site-Specific Performance

Site-specific performance, as a form of archaeological "excavation", can help to re-formulate how we perceive and experience space, place, and landscape. Centralia, as a now abandoned site characterized by ambiguity, unsettlement, and uncanny ambiance, can well serve as the "host" for site-specific performances.

Site-specific performance, as defined by Pearson and Shanks in their benchmark work, *Theatre/Archaeology (2001)*, state the following:

> *"Performance re-contextualizes such sites: it is the latest occupation of a location at which other occupations- their material traces and histories- are still apparent" (2001:23).*

Centralia, absent of social occupation and literally abandoned, with a popular vision that contradicts its past occupation as a community, warrants this re-contextualization. What better way to represent Centralia in the present (and future) than to use these other occupations and histories, and what remains, to portray the continuing "life" of the Centralia community.

But an active relationship, and not a passive vision, between performance and site must be open and fluid. Another important component of this relationship is that performance must be developed in relation to what occurred in the various occupations of residing in Centralia. The performance must be contextual to that history, not "another" popular one ("Hell on Earth").

A site-specific performance utilizes a site (such as Centralia) as "Host", that which remains (its occupational fixtures such as fragments of sidewalks), and that which is brought to the site during the "excavation" as performance (such as recorded sounds, historical dialogue, historical objects, and the recording devices). These performance "objects" become the "ghosts" of Centralia.

These remains and theatrical "props" (as "triggers") combine that which pre-exists at the site, and that which is part of an ethnographic immersion during the performance: combining the past and the present. The performance should resonate to the form (contextual acts that would have occurred there) and function (as a coal-mining community) of the site known as Centralia.

In these performances, we will utilize a rich overlay of narratives and experiences that combine memory, history, and sound. The nature of these performances will not be linear. Rather, we will use the material traces of what remains to create stories from history

This will involve acts of walking, looking, sensing, listening, and "excavating". The goal is to strip away layers of experience to recover and reveal what's left of Centralia, beneath the ruin. The absent physicality of the landscape will provide the history, stories, experiences, and the "ghosts".

In the performance, one is "ghosting" what may have happened in Centralia, in specific spaces, in the past. The idea is to use these performances in specific spaces as "excavation", a strategy of peeling back various layers (layer by layer), and "digging-deep" for what remains in particular historical layers. The "dig" is non-evasive, accomplished by contextual performances on the surface of the former spaces of the community.

The aim of this "excavation" is to enable multiple (and different) engagements to produce surface manifestations, allowing the space to remain open to remains that differ according to time, and the particular act of performance involved.

This is an exploration, a quest, for specific senses of presence past, and documenting their manifestations during the performance. What remains <u>and</u> manifests gives us a continuing sense of a place called Centralia. This is archaeological work. The use of performance seeks to represent, as an explanation, the ruin of history that has become the landscape of Centralia. It is working upon a relationship between past and present, in an attempt to turn performance and experience, "unearthing" what remains, into a contemporary representation, and more appropriate vision of Centralia.

In this respect, performance as "excavation" is both doing and something done. And as archaeology, it is both what remains of the past, and its manifestation in the present. If the past becomes present through our actions, that past is not dead, even when the visible remains are fragmented and in ruin. The past remains "alive" through our "excavating" acts upon it.

One sensory element that is particularly visceral in this performance as "excavation" is the use of sound, mentioned earlier in our soundscape surveys of Centralia. The development of a site soundscape, as we are recording in our surveys in Centralia, is as important for site-specific performances as the landscape itself.

Sound provides another form of site, apart from the physical. This is important in Centralia because it can encourage an audience to experience more of their surroundings (important in a place of absence); or, to view their surroundings differently (and away from the popular motif of a "Hell on Earth").

An example of a site-specific performance is the Weyburn Project, which uses the building founded as the Weyburn Mental Hospital in 1921 as the "Host" site. At the time, it was one of the largest buildings in the British Empire. Today, it is used for a number of community-based functions. The project used non-functioning areas of the hospital, which provided the history, legends, and the dreams that made up the eventual performance (in 2002). Weyburn is located in the province of Saskatchewan, Canada.

A similar site-specific event was conducted at an archaeological site in Central Greece, called Koutroulou Magoula, at the end of the excavation season. It included a theatrical performance, as well as communal feasting, music, and dance.

This event forms part of an "archaeological ethnography" (Hamilakis and Kyparissi-Apostolika 2011) that is meant to produce an active co-existence of multiple times, questioning the ontological stability of binary distinctions, such as past/present (among others).

But this particular performance was not about representing the past or conveying specific archaeological information. It was about presence. Performers did recall, evoke, and enact, however, various times and situations, without becoming empathetic to any one time or situation. In our fieldwork, however, we stress empathy, context, and resonance to a specific situation or act in a particular space.

The use of a site like Centralia is predicated on an understanding of the social, political, and economic factors that determined the form and function of the Centralia occupation. This calls into play, during the performances, of stories about the power of the coal barons, the dangers of coal mining, the ethnic conflicts, and the power of the Church in the lives of the Centralia community.

There is also the play of recreation, and the social life of the community that revolved around the importance of home, family, and social cooperation between people in Centralia in times of need. Site-specific performance as "excavation", then, is storytelling. But these stories must accommodate these different aspects of life in Centralia through time (as layered presence).

Centralia, contrary to popular belief, is <u>not</u> a "dead", forgotten, and deserted landscape. If the past lives on in the performances, and our memory of them, then there is more to be said and done in Centralia. We can return to re-visit what still remains in memory.

Let's make something more of these remains, rather than constructing a vision of "Hell on Earth"! In the process of "excavation", a site-specific performance has the potential to re-invigorate what little remains physically (and visibly) of Centralia!

Summary
Clearing the Field:
Re-Visualizing Centralia

There are many forms of archaeological excavation:

> *"Settings may vary from outside under the sun to the interior of caves to wreck sites deep under water. Different traditions of excavation, each with their own methods and techniques, are required...." (Edgeworth 2013:34).*

Today, an "excavation" can even mean a non-evasive "dig". Thinking of and analyzing absence is also the essence of an archaeological approach. As Harrison and Schofield recently suggested:

> *"No digging required. Just observe, engage, and think (2010:70).*

This is the **"process of archaeology as a particular sort of intervention and knowledge-making practice"** (Ibid: 116). This is archaeology as a performance, and is the sort of archaeological work that is ideal for a site like present-day Centralia.

In the "clearing" that is part of archaeological fieldwork, *"entities can emerge from the periphery of awareness at the fringes of the clearing or vanish back into the enclosing thicket again" ("Edgeworth 2013:34).*

This emergence and subsequent disappearance is a good example of what occurred at Centralia. The best way to experience the "clearing", according to Edgeworth, is **"to enter it....to try to make sense of unfolding evidence**

through working upon it…." (Ibid: 35). This is what we are trying to do with our proposed site-specific performances in Centralia.

In these performances, we literally get into or inhabit, in an embodied way, the material we are working with and on. This occurs during our acts of behavior that we do, and the objects we use, as we attempt to "clear" the spaces of former occupations.

The site of Centralia, like all archaeological sites, is hidden in what is still present, and what may emerge. A site, and its spaces to explore, is only disclosing fragments one at a time, offering traces in which one can continue to "excavate". In doing this work, there is a sense of expectation. It is an ever-present feeling of becoming, of something about to occur, and of material yet to emerge, as it manifests onto the former surfaces of occupation.

This is <u>not</u> a "paranormal" sense, something beyond comprehension and meaning. It is a common archaeological one, part of the recovery process. It is what haunts every archaeologist in the field. It is part of the archaeological way. It is not peculiar to Centralia because of what happened there. It <u>is</u> particular to Centralia because of what remains there: the amount and density of physical absence.

Every site that is opened up to archaeological intervention, and engaged with through contextual performance practices, is subject to a transforming potential in the course of fieldwork. But this transformation is based on what remains. It is not part of an imaginative or popular rendition of what people create in their own minds, or through their belief systems.

There is a warning here. What emerges here from this fieldwork should (must) not be taken up by others to "entertain" their <u>own</u> agendas. What emerges here is not intentionally political or economic. This fieldwork intervention is meant to be therapeutic and recuperative, to re-gain what has become lost in translation. It is meant as a remembrance and a memory of the Centralia its former residents once knew and loved so dearly!

Bibliography

Buchli, Victor and Gavin Lucas (2001). "The Archaeology of Alienation: A Late Twentieth-Century British Council House" in *Archaeologies of the Contemporary Past*. Victor Buchli and Gavin Lucas (Editors). London: Routledge. pp. 158-168.

DeKok, David (2010). *Fire Underground: The Ongoing Tragedy of the Centralia Mine Fire*. Guilford, Connecticut: Globe Pequot Press.

Edensor, T. (2005). *Industrial Ruins: Aesthetics, Materiality, and Memory*. Oxford: Berg.

Edgeworth, Matt. (2013). "The Clearing: Archaeological Way of Opening the World" in *Reclaiming Archaeology: Beyond the Tropes of Modernity*. Alfredo Gonzales Ruibal (Editor). London: Routledge. pp. 33-43.

Hamilakis,.Y and N. Kyparissi-Apostolika (2011). "Koutroulou Magoula". *British School at Athens, Annual Report 2009-2010*.

Harrison, Rodney and John Schofield (2010). *After Modernity: Archaeological Approaches to the Contemporary Past*. Oxford: Oxford University Press.

Heidegger, Martin.(1971).*On Time and Being*. New York: Harper & Rowe.

Lefebvre, Henri. (1992). *The Production of Space*. Maiden, Massachusetts: Blackwell Publishing.

Mann, Charles C. *(2006). 1491: New Revelations of the Americas Before Columbus*. New York: Vintage Books.

Pavis, P. (1998). Dictionary of the Theatre: Terms, Concepts, and Analysis. Toronto: University of Toronto Press.

Pearson, Mike. (2010). *Site-Specific Performance.* New York: Palgrave MacMillan.

Pearson, Mike and Michael Shanks. (2001). *Theatre/Archaeology.* London: Routledge.

Quigley, Joan. (2007). *The Day the Earth Caved In: An American Mining Tragedy. New York: Random House.*

Schneider, Rebecca. (2011). *Performing Remains: Art and War in Times of Theatrical Reenactment.* New York: Routledge.

Shanks, Michael. (2012). *The Archaeological Imagination.* Walnut Creek, California: Left Coast Press.

Thesing, William B. (2000). *Caverns of Night: Coal Mines in Art, Literature, and Film.* Columbia, South Carolina: University of South Carolina Press.

Tilley, Christopher. (1999). *Metaphor and Material Culture.* Oxford: Blackwell.

Author Biography

John Sabol is an archaeologist, cultural anthropologist, actor, and author. As an archaeologist, he has unearthed past material remains in excavations and site surveys in England, Mexico, and at various sites in the United States (including Eastern South Dakota, the Tennessee River Valleys, and in Pennsylvania). His anthropological fieldwork includes the studies of "spirits" in the religious beliefs of the afterlife among various cultural groups in Mexico (Mixtec, Zapotec, Lacandon, Nahuatl, and Otomi). His acting career includes "ghosting" performances of various characters and scenarios in more than 35 movies, TV shows, and documentaries. He has appeared in the A&E TV series, Paranormal State as an investigative consultant.

He has written sixteen books. These include: ***Ghost Excavator (2007), Ghost Culture (2007), Gettysburg Unearthed (2007), Battlefield Hauntscape (2008), The Anthracite Coal Region: The Archaeology of its Haunting Presence (2008), The Politics of Presence: Haunting Performances on the Gettysburg Battlefield (2008), Bodies of Substance, Fragments of Memories: An Archaeological Sensitivity to Ghostly Presence (2009), Phantom Gettysburg (2009), Digging Deep: An Archaeologist Unearths a Haunted Life (2009), The Re-Hauntings of Gettysburg (2010), Digging Up Ghosts (2011), The Haunted Theatre (2011), Haunting Archaeologies (2012), Beyond the Paranormal: Unearthing An Extended "Normal" at Haunted Locations (2013), Burnside Bridge Hauntscape: The Excavation of a Civil War Soundscape (2013), and The Gettysburg Battlefield Experience (2013).***

His recent speaking engagements include the T.A.G. (Theoretical Archaeology Group) Conference at the University of California, Berkeley, at the Space and Place Conference in Prague, Czech Republic, the TAG Conference at the University in Buffalo, New York, Exploring the Extraordinary Conference in York, England, the C.H.A.T. archaeological conference also in York, and the GHost Conference at the University of London, London, England.

His investigative reports have been published in such diverse venues as Haunted Times Magazine, Tennessee Anthropologist, and the online journal, ParaAnthropology. He has been a frequent guest on numerous radio and internet talk shows, among them, Beyond the Edge Radio, The Paranormal View, Para X Radio, Blog Talk Radio, The Grand Dark Conspiracy, and Rusty O'Nhiall's "Mysterious and Unexplained" on PsiFM (Australia). He was a university professor in Mexico for 11 years, teaching both undergraduate and graduate courses on the anthropology of tourism. He has also been featured on public educational TV for U.S. and foreign markets, and has worked on international educational documentaries (in Spain).

He has a M.A. in Anthropology/Archaeology (University of Tennessee), and a B.A. in Sociology/Anthropology (Bloomsburg University). He has also attended Penn State University, the University of Pittsburgh, the University of the Americas (Cholula, Puebla, Mexico), and has studied theatre and method acting in Mexico City.

He can be reached via email at cuicospirit@hotmail.com. His website is: **www.ghostexcavation.com** and he can be found on Facebook ("Ghost Excavations with John Sabol").

Photo 44: The Author During the Pioneer Tunnel Coal Mine Tour, Ashland, Pennsylvania.

Made in United States
Orlando, FL
28 December 2021